**Children's
Biography
MARQUETTE**

		DATE DUE		

Profiles in American History

The Life and Times of

FATHER JACQUES MARQUETTE

Mitchell Lane
PUBLISHERS

P.O. Box 196 · Hockessin, Delaware 19707

Profiles in American History

Titles in the Series

The Life and Times of

Abigail Adams
Alexander Hamilton
Benjamin Franklin
Betsy Ross
The Brothers Custer: Galloping to Glory
Clara Barton
Eli Whitney
Father Jacques Marquette
George Rogers Clark
Hernando Cortés
James Madison
John Adams
John Cabot
John Hancock
John Paul Jones
John Peter Zenger
Nathan Hale
Patrick Henry
Paul Revere
Peter Stuyvesant
Rosa Parks
Samuel Adams
Sir Walter Raleigh
Stephen F. Austin
Susan B. Anthony
Thomas Jefferson
William Penn

Profiles in American History

The Life and Times of

FATHER JACQUES MARQUETTE

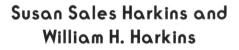

Susan Sales Harkins and
William H. Harkins

Printing   1   2   3   4   5   6   7   8   9

Library of Congress Cataloging-in-Publication Data
Harkins, Susan Sales.
    The life and times of Father Jacques Marquette / by Susan Sales Harkins and William H. Harkins.
        p. cm. — (Profiles in American history)
    Includes bibliographical references and index.
    Audience: Grades 7-8.
    ISBN 978-1-58415-528-7 (library bound)
    1. Marquette, Jacques, 1637–1675—Juvenile literature. 2. Explorers—America—Biography—Juvenile literature. 3. Explorers—France—Biography—Juvenile Literature. 4. Missionaries—Canada—Biography—Juvenile literature. 5. Canada—Discovery and exploration—Juvenile literature. 6. Canada—History—To 1763 (New France)—Juvenile Literature. 7. Mississippi River—Discovery and exploration—French—Juvenile literature. I. Harkins, William H. II. I. Title.
F1030.2.H37 2008
973.1'8092–dc22
[B]
                                                                        2007000793

ABOUT THE AUTHORS: Susan and William Harkins live in Kentucky, where they enjoy writing together for children. Susan has written many books for adults and children. William is a history buff. In addition to writing, he is a member of the Air National Guard. Susan and Bill have written several books for Mitchell Lane Publishers, including *The Life and Times of Clara Barton*, *The Life and Times of Pythagoras*, *What's So Great About King Tut?*, and *What's So Great About the Donner Party?*

AUTHORS' NOTE: The journal entries are written here as they appear in the sources listed. No corrections have been made to the spelling. The same is true for cited letters and other communications.

PUBLISHER'S NOTE: This story is based on the authors' extensive research, which they believe to be accurate. Documentation of such research is contained on page 46.
    The internet sites referenced herein were active as of the publication date. Due to the fleeting nature of some web sites, we cannot guarantee they will all be active when you are reading this book.

Profiles in American History

Contents

In 1673, Father Jacques Marquette took part in the adventure of a lifetime. He and his companions were the first white settlers to discover the source of the great Mississippi River. Their journals shared a view of several groups of Native Americans yet unknown to the Europeans. Their detailed maps opened the west for other explorers and traders.

CHAPTER
1

Men of Discovery

Huddled beneath buffalo robes, Father Jacques Marquette listened to the howling wind rip around his makeshift shack. Lying in the dim light that seeped through the snow-filled sky, Marquette prayed for an early spring. Sick from illness and the cold, he did little but sleep and pray. With frail hands, he rubbed the smooth beads of his rosary. The rote task gave him comfort, and for a while he let his mind wander to Kaskaskia and his native friends who waited for him to return. Of all the tribes he met along the Mississippi just a year earlier, the natives at Kaskaskia were the most eager to hear about his god.

In 1673, most of the North American continent was wilderness. Native peoples lived from coast to coast. Many were nomadic, following the animals they hunted for food or moving from season to season.

To the Europeans, who were beginning to settle there, what stretched beyond the east coast was a mystery—a dark, wild, and dangerous mystery. Brave men ventured into this wilderness. Some never returned. Perhaps they enjoyed the solitude and stayed. Or perhaps they chose to live with the natives. Many probably died alone and miserable. Few returned from their adventures with little more than furs and rumors.

The rumor that most interested the Europeans was the tale of a mighty river that flowed into a great sea. Natives called this river

the Father of Rivers. France, England, and Spain were still search-ing for the Northwest Passage—a water route through the North American continent to the Pacific Ocean. Was the Father of Rivers the Northwest Passage?

One hundred years earlier, Spanish explorer Hernando de Soto stumbled out of the southeastern forest and onto the banks of this great river. He named it Rio Grande, Spanish for "Big River." Other explorers eventually sailed down it into the Gulf of Mexico. They never explored the upper regions of the river. The Spanish stayed to the south, looking for gold and silver.

The English traveled inland from the Chesapeake Bay area. Falls or mountains always stopped them before they got very far.

The French explored the St. Lawrence River to the north. From their small settlement of Quebec, they traded with local natives for furs. Jesuit priests soon followed. Their goal was to convert the natives to Roman Catholicism.

One lone Jesuit missionary, Father Claude Allouez, ventured west, past today's Green Bay. Along the Fox River, he met Mascouten and Miami Indians. They talked of a great river named Messi-Sipi (Mississippi) that was only six days away.

The French began to suspect that the Spanish Rio Grande to the south and the Mississippi might be the same river. That is why an unlikely group of seven Frenchmen took the journey of a lifetime. The only way to solve the mystery of the great river was to find its source in the north and follow it south. Father Jacques Marquette and Louis Jolliet took that challenge.

The mission was dangerous. There were no European settlements along the way. They had no way of knowing where their journey would take them. They might never return.

Fear of the unknown didn't stop Father Marquette. When Jolliet, a French fur trader, first talked about the trip, the Jesuit priest was excited for him. Then Jolliet gave Father Marquette a letter from his superior, Father Claude Dablon. Father Dablon knew of Father Marquette's dream to preach to native peoples. Jolliet's search for the Mississippi could also help the young missionary fulfill his dream. In that letter, Father Dablon ordered Father Marquette to accompany Jolliet's group. (Some believe Father Marquette received his orders

Louis Jolliet was a true explorer. Traveling with Jolliet into the wilderness was the dream of a lifetime for Marquette. His goal was to convert the Native Americans to Christianity. His friendliness toward the native peoples along their river route, and his ability to speak with them, saved Jolliet's group many times.

from a visiting missionary, and not from Jolliet. However, the Jolliet meeting is the traditional story.)

On May 17, 1673, Father Marquette and Jolliet pushed two birchbark canoes into the water and paddled away from Father Marquette's home at the Saint Ignace mission. We can easily imagine Father Marquette waving farewell to his native friends on shore. He might never see them again.

Besides Father Marquette and Jolliet, the small group included a few Frenchmen: Jean Tiberge, Jacques Largillier, Pierre Moreau, and Jean Plattier. Two Indian guides agreed to accompany the group.

(Pierre Porteret, another Frenchman, may have been in the group, but sources disagree.)

Jolliet carried a compass and an astrolabe, a special instrument that used the sun to measure latitude. The men took few supplies: mostly dried meat, corn, and gifts for the natives they were sure to encounter. Father Marquette wrote of their preparations in his journal. "We were not long in preparing all our Equipment, although we were about to Begin a voyage, the duration of which we could not foresee. Indian Corn, with some smoked meat, constituted all our provisions; with these we Embarked—Monsieur Jollyet and myself, with 5 men—in 2 Bark Canoes, fully resolved to do and suffer everything for so glorious an Undertaking."[1]

The men took turns paddling the canoes. One man knelt at the front of the boat and paddled. From the back of the canoe, a second man used his paddle to steer.

At first, they kept to the northern shore of Lake Michigan. Weather was mild and they were happy to be on their way. "The Joy that we felt at being selected for This Expedition animated our Courage, and rendered the labor of paddling from morning to night agreeable to us."[2]

They traveled about thirty miles a day. The men used nets to fish for food. At night, they camped on shore. Soon they reached a bay they called Bay des Puants. Today it is called Green Bay.

In early June, Father Marquette paddled up the Menominee River to visit the Menominee Indians who lived there. Gliding through swamps, he carefully maneuvered the canoe through a shallow and muddy marsh. Slowly, he slid by the tall grain that grew on the banks.

When the friendly Menominee Indians heard of Father Marquette's journey, they warned him: Southern tribes were hostile. Terrible monsters lived in the great river. Father Marquette wrote about their warnings in his journal: "They represented to me that I would meet Nations who never show mercy to Strangers, but Break Their heads without any cause. . . . They also said that the great River was very dangerous . . . that it was full of horrible monsters, which devoured men and Canoes Together. . . . Finally that the Heat was so excessive In those countries that it would Inevitably Cause Our death."[3]

After a short visit, Father Marquette returned to his group. Soon, they reached the southern tip of the bay, where the men observed a tide. Following the bay's current, the canoes slipped into the Fox River. There, they visited with the missionaries at the Saint Francis-Xavier Jesuit mission. The men probably left the mission with mixed feelings. They were about to leave French territory behind.

Before reaching the Mississippi, Marquette and his companions traveled along shallow rivers and through swamps. Often, they had to carry their canoes and supplies. It wasn't a trip for the weak or timid.

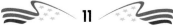

Back in the Fox River, the men struggled to guide their canoes around sharp rocks. Five times, they stopped to carry their canoes and supplies around dangerous rapids.

For a short time, the explorers left the Fox River for the shallow waters of Lake Winnebago. Their canoes glided through smelly swamps of tall reeds for almost twenty miles. Eventually, they reentered the Fox River. On June 7, they stopped at a Mascouten ("The Fire Nation") village. The Indians recognized Father Marquette as a priest because of his black robes, and they called him Blackrobe.

Father Marquette found the Indians gentle and pleasant. From their village of grass huts, the priest saw prairies on all sides. In the middle of the village, he found a huge cross. Together, the French explorers and the Mascouten chiefs smoked the calumet—a peace pipe.

On June 10, the Frenchmen left the Mascouten village, with two Miami guides who lived at the village. No Frenchman, and possibly no other European, had visited the lands west of the Mascouten village. They were probably excited and scared. The Indians they left behind also seemed to have misgivings about the journey, as noted by Father Marquette in his journal: "On the following day, the tenth of June, two Miamis who were given us as guides embarked with us, in the sight of a great crowd, who could not sufficiently express their astonishment at the sight of seven Frenchmen, alone and in two Canoes, daring to undertake so extraordinary and so hazardous an Expedition."[4]

About ten miles down the Fox River, the Miami guides led the small party to the shore. They carried their canoes and supplies over marshland for 2,700 paces (Father Marquette counted each step). On the other side of a narrow strip of land, the men found the Wisconsin River. The Frenchmen took the river south. Their Miami guides returned to their village.

The native guides had shown the French explorers a shortcut to the Wisconsin River, which would take them to the Mississippi River. Without the help of these guides, it is doubtful that the Frenchmen would have found their way through the maze of small rivers, lakes, and marshes that led from the Fox River into the Wisconsin River.

In unknown territory, the explorers were finally on their own. None of them knew what direction the river would take them.

Hernando de Soto

The Spanish were the first Europeans to explore the southern portion of the New World. In 1539, a small group of Spanish conquistadores, led by Hernando de Soto, explored Florida and Panama. They were infamous for burning the natives' villages after stealing their food. They took many slaves from among the native tribes. Instead of finding gold, they found mosquitoes, swamps, and alligators.

Discouraged, de Soto led his men west. They walked through dense forests and boggy marshes for two years. They went as far north as the Appalachian Mountains. They burned, pillaged, and murdered their way through today's Carolinas, Georgia, Alabama, and Mississippi.

On May 8, 1541, they stumbled out of the forest and upon a huge river flowing south. They named the river Rio Grande (Spanish for "Big River"). These men opted to cross the river instead of exploring it. There's no way to prove that de Soto's men were the first Europeans to see the Mississippi River. They are the first to document their sighting.

De Soto wasn't impressed with the wide river. It was just one more problem he had to solve. His 400 men would have to find a way across. It took them a month to build enough floats to make the crossing into today's Arkansas.

A year later, the explorers returned to the river, exhausted and sick. De Soto died on its banks. His men buried him, then sailed south on it to the Gulf of Mexico. From there, they sailed home to Mexico. Spain claimed the river that would become known as the Mississippi.

In Discovery of the Mississippi, *painted by William Powell in 1855, de Soto arrives at the great river in 1541.*

Domenico Quaglio created this painting of Reims Cathedral in 1833. New France and the western wilderness were nothing like Marquette's French home. He left behind a civilized and modern world full of every advantage: architecture, art, universities, theaters, and rich food and wine.

CHAPTER 2

From Pious Boy to Pious Priest

It's hard to imagine why anyone, let alone a Jesuit priest, would willingly venture into harm's way. For Father Marquette, the journey west to find the Mississippi River was a way to satisfy his lifelong dream. Since childhood, he had wanted to be a Jesuit missionary.

Jacques Marquette was a pious Catholic, even as a child. Religion was the cornerstone of his life. As a young boy, he knew he wanted to be a missionary. As a young priest, still living in France, he wrote to Father John Paul Oliva that he had yearned to be a missionary "from my earliest boyhood and the first light of reason."[1]

Nicolas Marquette and Rose de la Salle welcomed Jacques into the world on June 1 (or, according to some sources, June 10), 1637. The boy had two older sisters. Three brothers followed him. Like most French, the Marquettes were Roman Catholic.

The Marquette family was also prominent and wealthy. Marquettes had lived in Laon for at least 500 years. The family served the public. Jacques' ancestors were mayors, magistrates, treasurers, sheriffs, and judges. Nicolas Marquette was an important lawyer.

Servants kept the house in order, cooked the meals, and tended the children. Most likely, the children shared a common area, or nursery, in a second- or third-floor room. Their father probably worked from their home in a first-floor office. Because of his business

and his prominent position in society, important guests would have been common.

Jacques began his education around the age of five or six. Tradition holds that he took his early lessons with an uncle, who was also the pastor of his parish (most likely Nicolas' brother). Jacques used chalk and a piece of slate to practice his letters and sums.

At age nine (in 1646), Jacques traveled, probably by stagecoach, to Reims, France. There, he enrolled in one of France's seventy-seven Jesuit colleges. The Jesuit priests belonged to the order of The Society of Jesus, founded by Saint Ignatius Loyola. Originally, they acted as reformers against Islam. Later, they tried to stop the spread of Protestantism in Germany and France. From the beginning, their missionaries traveled far and wide: India, Japan, China, and later the New World.

Chalk and slate

The Jesuits promoted salvation and perfection. It was their hope that their students would share all they learned, both religious and academic, with the rest of society. They graduated young men with intelligent minds, sound judgment, and pious hearts.

Classes were year round, except for a three-week vacation each summer. The boys learned the basics of any traditional education of that time—mathematics and Latin, plus philosophy and Greek. By graduation, each student could read and write Greek and Latin. They could speak Latin fluently. While learning history, math, and geography, they read the classics. At about age fifteen, the boys began to study science, logic, and metaphysics.

Despite a strict schedule and intense study sessions, the Jesuits treated their students well. There was plenty of food, companionship, and leadership. In the winter, huge fires burned to keep the boys warm. Lamps lit each boy's desk as he studied on dark winter evenings. It was often cold, but it was the seventeenth century. The students would have been just as cold at home. Drafts were a condition of the time and technology, not a Jesuit punishment.

Classes were kept interesting with spirited discussions. The boys learned to reason, not just to memorize facts. Students competed in academic competitions and received awards for excellence.

One of their favorite activities was producing theatrical dramas. The Jesuits believed participating in the dramas helped the boys become poised public speakers.

The boys were well fed and indulged with physical outlets. Most boys fared well in the strict and well-supervised environment. Jacques certainly did.

Jacques' teacher during 1647 was Thierry Beschefer, a novitiate who wanted to be a missionary. He hoped to go to New France. Jacques had hoped to be a missionary for as long as he could remember, but he had imagined himself going to Asia. Most likely, this year with Beschefer changed Jacques' future. Eventually, Beschefer made it to New France, where he spent twenty-six years as a missionary. Later, he would request that Jacques join him in New France.

Jacques graduated from the Jesuit college in 1654. For eight years, he had lived with the Jesuits, spending only one month each year with his family in Laon. Upon graduation, at about age seventeen, Jacques earned a bachelor of arts degree.

Most of the graduates went on to study law, medicine and theology, but not Jacques. Just a few weeks after graduating, he entered the Jesuit novitiate at Nancy, France. Soon after arriving in October, he spent a month in seclusion. Like all Jesuit novitiates, or novices, he spent this month contemplating his spiritual journey and praying.

His days as a Jesuit novice were more intense and regulated than his school days had been. Cooking, mopping floors, doing laundry, and gardening were all new experiences for him. Jacques spent a month in a hospital nursing the sick. During the seventeenth century, hospitals were little more than houses of death. No one went to the hospital to get well. They went to the hospital to die. During this time, Jacques cleaned and tended to the ill. He even dug graves.

All novices were required to take a monthlong pilgrimage. They left the novitiate with no money. They begged for food and shelter. Jacques made his pilgrimage during his second year at the novitiate. He and another novice walked from Nancy to Trier and back—a 200-mile round-trip.

The trip was physically demanding and humbling, and that was its purpose. Many novices, like Jacques, were from prominent and wealthy families. Begging for food was probably difficult. During their pilgrimage, they learned to trust God to provide for their needs. Perhaps more important, they saw how most people, the people they would be serving, lived.

After two years of this training, Jacques took his vows. He began his career as a scholastic—a college-level student preparing for ordination—at the Jesuit college in Auxerre, France. The school was small, with eleven priests, five Brothers, and only one other scholastic besides Jacques. After one year at the small college, Marquette left for Pont-à-Mousson, where he studied philosophy.

During his second year of philosophical study, Marquette requested a foreign mission. He was still young, and the Jesuits liked their missionaries to have more education and more experience. Marquette would have to wait. Instead of traveling to China or Japan, he returned to Reims to teach.

Between 1661 and 1665, Marquette taught at several different colleges throughout France. At this point in their careers, most priests finished their study of philosophy and then advanced to theology. More study wasn't the future Marquette wanted. In March of 1665, he wrote to Jesuit John Paul Oliva, explaining that he hoped to receive a foreign mission soon. He no longer cared where he went; he was prepared to go wherever they sent him.

About this time, Marquette's previous teacher, Father Beschefer, requested that Jacques join him in Quebec. After being ordained on March 7, 1666, Marquette left his teaching position and traveled to La Rochelle. There, he boarded a ship for Quebec.

Like most sea voyages of that time, the passengers suffered. Within days, everyone had lice. Food was barely edible. Certainly there was nothing with any real nutritional value, and before long, passengers were sick with scurvy. Father Marquette spent the voyage nursing the sick passengers and crew. After a grueling six-week journey over the treacherous and stormy North Atlantic, Father Marquette arrived in Quebec on September 20, 1666.

Pilgrimage

Father Marquette made his first pilgrimage long before he was a priest. He was just a child of six when the French King, Louis XIII, lay dying in Saint-Germain-en-Laye, France. That May, all of France prayed for his recovery. A story, passed down through the generations, describes young Jacques taking a pilgrimage to Notre Dame de Liesse with his family.

King Louis XIII

Pilgrimages were common during this time. They were long journeys, for different reasons, but usually religious or spiritual ones. Often, a pilgrimage was a visit to a religious shrine or a sacred place. Pilgrimages were solemn occasions.

Laon's bishop of the day, Benjamin de Brichanteau, organized a pilgrimage to de Liesse to pray for Louis XIII. The pilgrims from Laon, including Jacques and his family, walked the entire eight miles.

Everyone in Jacques' family probably made the pilgrimage. They would have walked slowly. As they walked, they would have prayed and sung. They would have said the rosary (a Catholic ritual of prayer and penance) as they walked. It is hard to imagine such a small child making such a long journey on foot. Perhaps Jacques' older sisters or his father carried him when he got too tired to walk.

Praying at the sanctuary of Our Lady of Liesse

At Liesse, the pilgrims kneeled before the statue of Our Lady, where they prayed to her for their king. The shrine was sacred to the citizens of Laon, who believed that angels carried the statue from Jerusalem to Laon during the eleventh century.

Despite the best efforts of his pious subjects, Louis XIII died on May 14, 1643.

For Your Information

Father Jacques Marquette and his companions left his Mackinac Island mission (in modern-day Michigan) to find the Northwest Passage. They discovered the Mississippi River instead.

CHAPTER
3

New France

Quebec's harbor on the St. Lawrence River was busy when Father Marquette arrived. Six ships were unloading goods for the settlers and loading furs for the return trip to France. Most likely, Father Beschefer met Marquette at the dock. They would have used hand-carts to carry Father Marquette's luggage through town.

Father Marquette walked through a small but thriving village to the mission. In the lower town by the dock, small wooden shops filled with tailors, tinsmiths, and bakers lined the narrow mud streets. By New World standards, the settlement was successful, with 547 people and fifty businesses (according to the first census, taken in 1666).[1]

Men called voyageurs, dressed in leather and knitted stocking caps, walked the streets with fur pelts thrown over their shoulders. These traders helped move men and supplies from the harbor to the more remote settlements. Soldiers, on and off duty, walked through town. It would have been difficult for Father Marquette to tell the soldiers from anyone else because they wore ordinary work clothes instead of colorful uniforms. There were few horses—nearly everyone walked.

That day, Father Marquette probably got his first look at natives. Wearing beaded buckskins and leather leggings, natives were common in Quebec. Although the Spanish and English often clashed

with the natives, the French didn't. The French were fur traders. Some French adventurers did trap, but the natives were superior at it. Instead of trapping, the French traded for furs with the natives. They learned the native languages, and married into their tribes. In the early years of the seventeenth century, the French built a profitable trading business, aided by the Indians.

Father Marquette learned about the colony quickly. Jacques Cartier first claimed Quebec for France in 1534, but it was Samuel de Champlain who built the first fort in 1608. Soon, the small community was the capital of New France. Other communities, such as Three Rivers and Montreal, depended on Quebec's harbor. Each spring, trappers and traders from all over New France disappeared into the wilderness to collect or trade for pelts. Eventually, they all made their way to Quebec to turn in their bundles.

Jacques Cartier discovered and explored the St. Lawrence River. Later, Samuel de Champlain followed Cartier's route up the St. Lawrence and established the first permanent settlement at Quebec.

It wasn't long before the French missionaries made the trip to New France. Believing that Roman Catholicism was the only true religion, they came to convert the natives. Spurred by their initial successes with the Huron and Algonquin Indians, the Jesuits hoped to move westward. That's why Father Marquette had come to New France. He was going to travel west to establish a new mission. It was a dangerous undertaking that could cost him his life. Father Marquette didn't let the danger stop him. He wanted to go.

Outside the mission, Father Marquette soon felt the tense relations between the Jesuits and the colony's officials. New France was a crown colony, but run by the Company of the West Indies. The company's goal was to make a profit. Furs, especially beaver furs, provided the colony's main income. European craftsmen turned the beaver pelts into felt hats and other goods, which were extremely popular at this time.

Most of the furs came from the natives. The company's representatives traded European goods for pelts. Some traders deceived the natives, and the Jesuits objected to the practice. Traders and civil authorities argued that the Jesuits wanted to control the colony.

In October, Father Marquette traveled to Three Rivers, another French settlement on the St. Lawrence River. There, he ministered to the Algonquin Indians. Many were already Christian converts living near the mission. The Algonquins at the mission taught Father Marquette how to speak their native tongue. He taught them how to speak French.

Only after Father Marquette was fluent in Algonquian did the Jesuits allow him to travel west to the Great Lakes. He made the voyage of 1,500 miles with some Ottawa Indians from that region who were traveling home.

Father Marquette started his mission in a small settlement on the St. Mary's River between Lake Huron and Lake Superior. Chippewa Indians and French traders already lived in the area they called the Sault (pronounced *soo*). He called the new mission Sault Sainte Marie.

Immediately, Father Marquette began to minister to the Chippewa. He wasn't just a priest in the spiritual sense, either. He gave comfort and assistance in any way he could. He nursed the sick and lent

comfort to anyone in need. The Chippewa welcomed him into their homes.

While Father Marquette spent time with the Chippewa, three other Jesuits built the mission. They erected a log house, a small chapel, and even a barn. To secure the mission, they raised a wall of twelve-foot posts. That way the mission could serve as a fort if necessary.

Other tribes often came to the river to fish. Father Marquette took advantage of these visits. He learned many words in several native languages. He also learned their sign language. Soon, he was preaching to the Chippewa, the Miami, the Cree, and the Illinois people.

Father Jacques Marquette had one dream—to convert the native peoples in the New World to Christianity. Whether he converted many isn't known. We do know that he was kind to them, and they in turn respected the priest they called Blackrobe.

It was at his small mission at Sault Sainte Marie that Father Marquette heard of the great river, the Mississippi. Local Ottawa Indians kept a Shawnee slave, who described a great river near his home. From his village, the river that flowed north to south was just a five-day journey.

That spring (1669), two Jesuit visitors brought news from Quebec. Father Marquette was to move even farther west to Saint Esprit on the southern shore of Lake Superior. He left in August, but it was already cold on the lake. Snow and ice slowed their trip. It took a month for the travelers to reach Saint Esprit.

He stayed at Saint Esprit, with the Ottawa and Huron Indians, for a year. Besides acting as their priest, he hunted and fished with them. It was a peaceful and joyful time for Father Marquette.

He also heard more about the Mississippi River. The local Ottawas allowed Father Marquette to care for a young Illinois captive. Father Marquette taught the boy French, and the boy taught the priest how to speak his language. The boy spoke of a great river that flowed north to south.

The peace at the mission was broken when war broke out in the spring of 1671. Bands of Sioux Indians raided the settlement. Father Marquette and the natives at the mission loaded their canoes and fled eastward. They settled at Michilimackinac between Lake Huron and Lake Michigan. He called their new home Saint Ignace. They lived well and peacefully for another year.

Once again, unexpected visitors brought news that would change Father Marquette's life. Louis Jolliet, a French fur trader, handed Father Marquette a letter from his Jesuit superior, Father Claude Dablon. That letter ordered Father Marquette to join Jolliet on his westward journey to find the Mississippi River. It was the chance of a lifetime for both men. They spent the fall and spring preparing for and planning the trip.

Finally, on May 17, 1673, they left the small mission of Saint Ignace and traveled southwest. From May to mid-June, the small group of French explorers paddled their canoes through the rivers, bays, and marshes of the Great Lakes area. With the help of two Miami guides, they found the Wisconsin River.

Buffalo grazed along the plains of the Mississippi River. Father Jacques Marquette and his companions had never seen them before. With plenty of game and fish, the group never went hungry.

The Wisconsin River was full of small islands and difficult to navigate. The sandy bottom constantly shifted. The canoes often ran aground. Despite their difficulties, the explorers enjoyed the scenery. The river flowed through forests and prairies. They saw animals and trees they had never seen before. At night, they saw grazing herds of buffalo. Father Marquette called them cattle. Soon, the water deepened and the boats began to glide easily over the surface of the water. Perhaps, they hoped, the Mississippi was close.

The Government of New France

Twenty years before Father Marquette arrived in Quebec, a small group of men ruled New France. That group included the governor, a religious leader, the head of the Jesuits, and the governor of Montreal.

In 1663, King Louis XIV of France did away with the council. He entrusted the colony to the Company of the West Indies. France was a royal province, but the company ran the colony.

King Louis XIV

Under the new company, three people controlled New France—a governor, an intendant, and a bishop. The governor handled the colony's defense. An intendant took care of the colony's internal affairs. Mostly, he spent the colony's money. He also ran the colony's judicial system. Any colonial police force was his responsibility. The bishop administered mission work and led the church.

The first intendant, Jean Talon, brought thousands of settlers to New France. He was responsible for Father Marquette and Louis Jolliet's expedition to find the Mississippi River.

Jean Talon

Most officials were wealthy. Social arrogance and abuse of power were widespread. Council members fought over imaginary insults and social standing.

Despite the fighting, the company was prosperous in New France, but not elsewhere. By the time Father Marquette and Jolliet made their trip down the Mississippi, the company was in debt. The king canceled the company's charter in 1674 and paid the company's debt. At that, all colonies stretching from Newfoundland to Louisiana came under the king's direct control.

Marquette and Jolliet, carved on the Michigan Avenue Bridge in Chicago, created in 1928. The explorers met many friendly natives during their journey. They always stopped, shared a meal, and exchanged gifts. Often, they spent a few days with the natives. Always, they asked about the great waterway to the west.

CHAPTER 4

"We Entered Missisipi . . ."[1]

On June 17, the canoes rounded a small island and the men got their first glimpse of the Mississippi River. It was an incredible sight—the Mississippi was a mile across. They watched the two rivers flow into one and allowed the current to guide their canoes from the Wisconsin River into the Mississippi.

It seemed to the men that the Mississippi River held more water than all the rivers of Europe. Today, we know that the Mississippi River watershed comprises 35,000 miles of rivers.

For those first few days, the weather was mild and the current was gentle. The canoes slipped past marshes, coves, and islands that split the river into channels. Except for the strange fish and animals they encountered, this part of the trip was uneventful. "From time to time, we came upon monstrous fish, one of which struck our Canoe with such violence that I Thought that it was a great tree, about to break the Canoe to pieces. On another occasion, we saw on The water a monster with the head of a tiger, a sharp nose Like That of a wildcat, with whiskers and straight, Erect ears; The head was gray and The neck quite black . . ."[2]

Eventually, the woods and cliffs gave way to open prairie on both sides. The explorers stopped to hunt. Afterward, they ate buffalo and wild turkey. Father Marquette found the buffalo hideous to look at, but delicious, as noted in his journal: "The flesh and the fat

Father Jacques Marquette and Louis Jolliet were the first known European explorers to discover, explore, and map the upper Mississippi River.

of the pisikious [bison] are Excellent, and constitute the best dish at feasts."[3]

Because they were in unknown territory, they slept in their rocking canoes anchored far off shore. They kept watch all night.

On June 25, eight days after entering the Mississippi River, they saw a small path leading from the water's edge into the prairie. Father Marquette and Jolliet left their canoes and the other men at the riverbank and followed the path. After a few hours, they found a native village. The two men, alone in the wilderness, were so close they could hear the natives talking to one another. They shouted to

alert the natives to their presence. It was a brave thing to do. There was no way to know how the natives might react.

Four older men approached them. One held a pipe decorated with white feathers. Father Marquette recognized it as a peace pipe. He spoke to them and they understood him. They replied that they were Illinois Indians and invited the white men to smoke the peace pipe.

Villagers greeted the Frenchmen warmly, as Father Marquette wrote in his journal: "At the door of the Cabin . . . was an old man . . . This man stood erect, and stark naked, with his hands extended and lifted toward the sun . . . he paid us This Compliment: 'How beautiful the sun is, O Frenchman, when thou comest to visit us! All our village awaits thee, and thou shalt enter all our Cabins in peace.' "[4]

Sitting cross-legged, the two Frenchmen smoked the peace pipe again with their new Illinois friends. The pipe had a polished red bowl made of stone. Bird skulls and colorful feathers hung from the pipe's two-foot-long stem.

Jolliet gave presents to the Illinois. Then the chief gave Jolliet a young slave boy. To Father Marquette, the chief gave a peace pipe. He begged the Frenchmen not to travel farther south because of the great dangers they faced. Since they insisted on going, he told them to present the pipe when meeting natives along their journey. Its power would protect them. Father Marquette wrote about the Illinois' respect for the peace pipe in his journal: "It has but to be carried upon one's person and displayed, to enable one to walk safely through the midst of Enemies—who, in the hottest of the Fight, lay down Their arms when it is shown. For that reason, the Illinois gave me one, to serve as a safeguard among all the Nations through whom I had to pass during my voyage."[5]

They ate sagamite—boiled corn mush seasoned with fat—fish, and wild ox at a feast. One of the Illinois men fed a few bites of each dish to both Father Marquette and Jolliet. Both of the Frenchmen politely declined the roast dog.

Father Marquette found the Illinois people gentle, amiable, and in good health. Their cabins were large. Rushes topped the huts and covered the dirt floors. The men were mostly naked, while the women wore animal skins.

The men each had several wives, but they were jealous of them. Husbands cut off the noses and ears of wives who were unfaithful.

After a few days in the village, the two Frenchmen returned to the river. Nearly 600 Illinois walked with them. These French explorers were the first white men most of them had ever seen. Father Marquette tried to leave the young boy, but the chief insisted that the boy go. (Some sources refer to this boy as the chief's son, but he was a slave. The chief referred to him as "my son" because he had adopted him in the native fashion.)

Back on the river, they saw monsters painted on rocks on a high bluff. Each monster had horns, the head of a deer, and the face of a man, with red eyes and a beard. A long tail wound around the body, which was covered in scales.

About this time, they heard a low roaring sound. It grew louder and louder as they continued south. Before they could react, their canoes plunged into a torrential rapid formed by a huge river from the west emptying into the Mississippi. They watched the gentle green waters of the Mississippi churning brown with the mud of the powerful tributary. They were passing the rapids at today's Cairo, Illinois, where the Missouri flows into the Mississippi. "I have seen nothing more dreadful,"[6] Marquette wrote in his journal.

Just a few days later, they passed the Ohio to the east. There, the green water of the Ohio mixed with the Mississippi's muddy waters.

The Mississippi grew in size and strength as it surged south. The weather grew warm and then hot. Soon, the men were sunburned. They were unaccustomed to hot weather.

A good wind blew most of the time, so they used canvas stretched over masts as sails and let the wind propel them. Mosquitoes from the swamps were bothersome, so they created tents of sailcloth. The tents protected them from the mosquitoes and the blazing sun.

Where the Arkansas River joins the Mississippi, the Frenchmen encountered angry natives on shore. Warriors with weapons ran along the riverbank. The noises they made terrified the Frenchmen. A few warriors tried to swim out to the canoes. At the same time, a canoe full of angry warriors paddled toward the explorers. It is possible that the warriors meant to kill them.

Father Marquette, in his black robe, stood up in the middle of his canoe. He shouted to them in Huron, and held the peace pipe high in the air. The natives didn't understand the Huron, but the Illinois chief had been right. Seeing the peace pipe, a couple of the older men on shore called to the warriors. It took a few minutes to calm the young men, but they respected the older men and obeyed.

Before entering the Mississippi, a friendly native chief gave Father Marquette a peace pipe. It may have saved their life, more than once. As the small group paddled toward unknown natives on the shore, Marquette would hold out the peace pipe for all to see.

Eventually, the group welcomed the white explorers and shared a meal with them.

They were members of the Quapaw nation. Father Marquette tried to speak to them using several native languages. Finally, an older man understood the priest when he spoke Illinois.

Jolliet presented the Quapaw Indians with knives, hatchets, and beads. Father Marquette asked about their guns. The natives didn't create metal tools. Guns, hatchets, and knives were acquired through trade with Europeans. The Quapaw explained that they traded with Europeans to the east. Father Marquette and Jolliet wondered if they were in Spanish lands—enemy territory.

They also learned that they were just days from the great sea. It was clear now that the Mississippi River must flow south to the Gulf of Mexico. Their trip downriver was almost over, and they knew it.

The next day, the Quapaw took the French explorers farther south to another Quapaw village. The friendly people of Akamsea welcomed them. Like so many native men, the Quapaw men were naked. Most men had pierced noses and ears. The women wore animal skins.

As was customary, the travelers shared a meal with the villagers, and Jolliet passed out gifts. The Quapaw talked of the Europeans who lived at the mouth of the river. Hearing this, Father Marquette and Jolliet knew their trip was over. They must be deep in Spanish territory if the mouth of the Mississippi was just a few days away.

Fearing the Spanish would capture them if they went any farther south, Father Marquette and Jolliet decided it was time to return home. It was July 17, and after traveling 1,100 miles, they set their course north for home.

Monuments along the rivers of the north commemorate the voyage of Father Jacques Marquette and Louis Jolliet.

The Birchbark Canoe

Early European explorers used different types of canoes to explore rivers. French explorers depended on lightweight canoes made of birchbark, which were good for exploring. The Spanish used huge dugout canoes made from the trunks of cottonwood trees that could carry fifty warriors. Both were based on native designs. English explorers used a type of small boat of European design, called a shallop.

Paper birch tree

The French got their design from the northeastern natives, who used the bark of the paper birch tree (*Betula papyrifera*) to make their canoes. In late fall or early spring, they peeled the bark from the trees. They rolled the bark strips into bundles, which they carried back to their villages. While the strips of bark were still fresh and pliable, they wrapped them around the canoe's framework, made from white cedar wood tied together with rawhide. As the bark dried, it took on the shape of the framework. Later, they filled cracks and holes with resin from the white spruce.

The birchbark canoe was the best design for exploring. It was easy to maneuver in water and light enough to carry across land. Camping on land at night, the men rested their canoes upside down on poles and slept under them. Larger versions of the same design were used to carry cargo. The French explorers used the birchbark canoes to explore the marshes, bays, and rivers of the Great Lakes region. Traders used them to travel between trading posts and their native trading partners. Father Marquette and Jolliet used these canoes to find and explore the Mississippi River.

The paper birch tree doesn't grow along the southern Mississippi, which probably explains why the native peoples and explorers to the south did not use them.

During the voyage home, Father Marquette grew ill. He never fully recovered and died just a few days before his thirty-eighth birthday.

CHAPTER 5

The Trip Home and More

Paddling against the current the entire way, the men found the long journey home demanding. They labored past the strong waters of the Ohio and Missouri Rivers as they poured into the Mississippi. They decided to take the Illinois River northeast. It was a shorter route to Lake Michigan, according to the Illinois people.

Along the Illinois River, they stopped at Kaskaskia and smoked the peace pipe. Father Marquette preached, and promised to return to the village. Perhaps he would start a mission at Kaskaskia. His journal suggests that the Illinois were eager for him to return. "We found on it a village of Illinois called Kaskaskia, consisting of 74 Cabins. They received us very well, and obliged me to promise that I would return to instruct them."[1]

By the end of September, they were back at the Saint Francis-Xavier mission. They had been gone four months and, including the many smaller tributaries the group had explored, had paddled 2,900 miles.

Father Marquette remained at Saint Francis-Xavier. For weeks, he'd been sick with a fever, stomach cramps, and diarrhea. Most likely, he was suffering from dysentery or typhoid fever. That cold winter, Father Marquette lived at the mission and rewrote his journal. He also worked on a map of the Mississippi River and its tributaries.

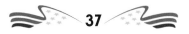

Jolliet returned to the mission at Sault Sainte Marie. Some experts believe he spent the winter with Marquette, using the time to make a copy of his journal. Unfortunately, the mission caught fire and Jolliet's copy and maps of the journey were lost.

The next spring, Jolliet headed for Montreal, traveling by river. Along the way, the canoe capsized. Two of his men and the young native boy, whom Jolliet had grown to love as a son, drowned. His original journal was gone.

Father Marquette was still at Saint Francis-Xavier, hoping to return to the Illinois. He was just too sick. Other Jesuits nursed him through the spring and summer of 1674. By fall, Father Marquette was somewhat better, and he insisted on taking a trip to see the Illinois. With the help of Jacques Largillier and Pierre Porteret, he left Saint Francis-Xavier on October 25, 1674, bound for Kaskaskia.

Along the way, the three men joined a large group of Illinois Indians traveling the same direction. At night, while they sat around the campfires, Father Marquette preached.

Bad weather slowed the group. Father Marquette grew ill again. His fever was high. Lake Michigan froze, and the men dodged floating chunks of ice as they paddled. Close to the banks of the Chicago River (near today's Chicago, Illinois), the river was frozen. The group built a shelter on shore.

Fortunately, game was plentiful. Buffalo robes, for which they traded, kept them warm. Illinois friends and other French traders knew of their camp and sent provisions. That winter passed slowly. Father Marquette did not get well.

Once the river opened in March, the small group left their winter shelter. After a bitterly cold journey, they finally arrived at Kaskaskia on April 10, 1675.

The Illinois were glad to see Blackrobe again. The next day, he held an Easter Mass. Afterward, he gave gifts to the chiefs. Father Marquette's visit was short, since he was due at Saint Ignace. He had planned to spend the entire winter with the Illinois. Instead, he'd spent the winter in a makeshift lean-to surrounded by snow and ice.

As a show of respect, the Illinois escorted Father Marquette upriver for eleven days. At Lake Michigan, the Illinois turned back.

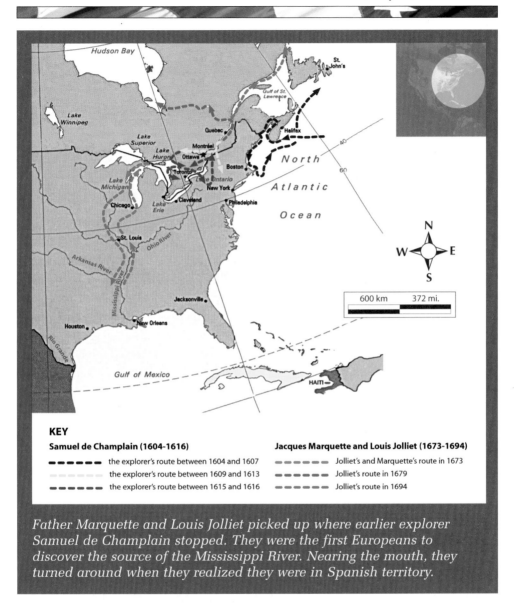

KEY

Samuel de Champlain (1604-1616)

▬ ▬ ▬ ▬ ▬ the explorer's route between 1604 and 1607

▬ ▬ ▬ ▬ ▬ the explorer's route between 1609 and 1613

▬ ▬ ▬ ▬ ▬ the explorer's route between 1615 and 1616

Jacques Marquette and Louis Jolliet (1673-1694)

▬ ▬ ▬ ▬ ▬ Jolliet's and Marquette's route in 1673

▬ ▬ ▬ ▬ ▬ Jolliet's route in 1679

▬ ▬ ▬ ▬ ▬ Jolliet's route in 1694

Father Marquette and Louis Jolliet picked up where earlier explorer Samuel de Champlain stopped. They were the first Europeans to discover the source of the Mississippi River. Nearing the mouth, they turned around when they realized they were in Spanish territory.

By this time, Father Marquette was too weak to walk. The two traders paddled while Father Marquette lay in the middle of the canoe. Wrapped warmly, he didn't stir much. Occasionally, he moaned in pain.

On May 18, Father Marquette asked to stop. The traders carried the priest ashore. He spoke a few words just before he died. He was

only thirty-seven years old. His companions buried him near a river, which we know today as the Pere Marquette (*pere* is French for *father*).

In 1677, a band of Ottawa Indians found the grave. They dug up their beloved priest's bones. After cleaning and drying the remains, they laid them in a birchbark box. A large group of thirty canoes made the journey to Saint Ignace to return the remains to the mission. The Jesuits laid the bones to rest in a vault beneath the mission floor.

Excavators removed pieces of birchbark and bone from this grave in 1877. Later, in 1882, the Marquette Monument Association erected a monument at the site. They placed a few bone fragments from the original grave under the monument. Marquette University received the rest of the bone fragments. The original grave had no marker and was difficult to find. There's no evidence that either set of bones was actually the body of Father Jacques Marquette. The birchbark mixed with the bone fragments is evidence enough for most.

Father Marquette's role in the Mississippi River's story is heroic. We don't know how successful Jolliet's group would have been without Father Marquette. His gentleness and respect for the native peoples and their cultures endeared him to them. They learned quickly that the group was friendly. Father Marquette was able to ask questions about the river and the people who lived along it. That information was vital to their mission. He was the only member of the group who could speak so many native languages.

A few years after the priest's death, another Frenchman completed the journey that Father Marquette and Jolliet began. In 1666, Robert Cavelier de La Salle first heard of the river from the Seneca Indians who lived near his farm in Montreal. In December of 1681, La Salle started for the Mississippi. His purpose for the trip was to claim the river for France.

Two months later, La Salle entered the Mississippi. It was February, and chunks of ice floated in the river. Early in April, the great river branched into three channels. They were flowing between what are now the states of Louisiana and Mississippi. On April 9, the group crossed Lake Pontchartrain and into the Gulf of Mexico. La Salle named the region Louisiana after King Louis XIV.

The French claimed the entire Mississippi Valley. As a result, French territory stretched from the Appalachian Mountains to the Rockies and from the Gulf of St. Lawrence to the Gulf of Mexico. French traders settled along the Mississippi River. They built trading posts, which they also used as forts. Many towns along the river still reveal their French heritage in their architecture, food, and customs.

In 1699, the French sailed into the Gulf of Mexico and up the Mississippi, where they settled in what is now Ocean Springs, Mississippi. The French split Spain's territory by settling the Mississippi Valley.

In 1803, President Thomas Jefferson bought the Louisiana Territory for 15 million dollars. The French emperor, Napoleon Bonaparte, was at war with Europe. He didn't have the manpower or the money to defend his North American territory. Selling Louisiana to the United States was a good solution for everyone. The United States doubled its size with the Louisiana Purchase. Bonaparte used the money to continue his war.

Father Marquette and Louis Jolliet were a part of the French expansion, just as much as La Salle. They also expanded our knowledge of the native tribes along their route: Mascouten, Miami, Kiskabou, Illinois, Chickasaw, Akamsea, and Michigamea.

Centuries later, we credit Father Marquette and Louis Jolliet for solving the mystery of the Mississippi River. To the people that knew him, Father Marquette was much more than an explorer. After Father Marquette's death, his superior, Father Dablon, wrote of him: "We might say much of the rare virtues of this noble missionary: of his Zeal, which prompted him to carry the faith so far, and proclaim the gospel to so many peoples who were unknown to us; of his gentleness, which rendered him beloved by all, and made him all things to all men—a Frenchman with the French, a huron with the hurons, an Algonquin with the algonquins; of the childlike Candor with which he disclosed his heart to his superiors, and even to all kinds of person, with an ingenuousness which won all Hearts; of his angelic Chastity; and of his uninterrupted union with God."[2]

Jesuits—The Other Side

Much of what we know about Father Marquette comes from the journal he kept about his Mississippi River adventure. He comes across as gentle, honest, and respectful of the native peoples he met along the way.

This is not the picture many of Father Marquette's contemporaries had of the Jesuits. Traders and colony officials were often in conflict with the Jesuits. Civil officials, especially, accused the Jesuits of wanting to control the colony.

The Jesuits' goal was to convert the natives to Roman Catholicism. They had a reputation for being disruptive and harsh with the natives.

The natives had their own religion, which the Jesuits did not understand or respect. Showing their disdain for the religion the natives practiced did not subdue the natives; it just made enemies. For example, Father Claude Allouez, the same priest who paddled west to the Fox River, found the natives indecent. The Hurons in the area didn't think much of him either, as noted in the priest's own writings: "The slight esteem in which they held me caused them to steal every article of my wardrobe that they could, and I had trouble keeping my hat, the wide rim of which seemed to them well suited against the heat of the sun."[3]

His mission failed. The Huron did not care for his new religion. They liked him even less. Eventually, Father Allouez abandoned the mission when the natives refused to offer him food or shelter.

In contrast, from his early missionary days, Father Marquette found the natives friendly. They valued his friendship and treated him with respect. Whether they honored his religion, we don't know. They did honor him as a man. His journal implies it, through the generous and loving descriptions of the people he encountered. Any doubts of the native population's respect for the priest were laid to rest with the priest's bones.

Statue at Pere Marquette Park along Milwaukee Riverwalk

42

Chapter Notes

Chapter 1. Men of Discovery

1. Jacques Marquette, *Voyages of Marquette in The Jesuit Relations*, 59 (Ann Arbor: Ann Arbor University Microfilms, Inc., 1966), p. 91.
2. Ibid., p. 91.
3. Ibid., p. 95–97.
4. Ibid., p. 105.

Chapter 2. From Pious Boy to Pious Priest

1. Joseph P. Donelly, S.J., *Jacques Marquette, S.J.* (Chicago: Loyola University Press, 1968), p. 19.

Chapter 3. New France

1. Joseph P. Donelly, S.J., *Jacques Marquette, S.J.* (Chicago: Loyola University Press, 1968), p. 67.

Chapter 4. "We Entered Missisipi . . ."

1. Jacques Marquette, *Voyages of Marquette in The Jesuit Relations, 59* (Ann Arbor: Ann Arbor University Microfilms, Inc., 1966), p. 107.
2. Ibid., pp. 111–113.
3. Ibid., p. 113.
4. Ibid., pp. 117–119.
5. Ibid., pp. 130–131.
6. Ibid., p. 141.

Chapter 5. The Trip Home and More

1. Jacques Marquette, *Voyages of Marquette in The Jesuit Relations, 59* (Ann Arbor: Ann Arbor University Microfilms, Inc., 1966), p. 161.
2. Ibid., p. 207.
3. Ted Morgan, *Wilderness Dawn: The Settling of the North American Continent* (New York: Simon & Shuster, 1993), pp. 194–195.

Chronology

1637	Jacques Marquette is born in Laon, France on June 1.
1643	He and his family make a pilgrimage to Notre Dame de Liesse to pray for the dying King Louis XIII.
1646	Jacques enrolls in the Jesuit college at Reims.
1647	He has Thierry Beschefer for a teacher at the Jesuit college. This priest later requests that Marquette join him in New France.
1654	Marquette graduates from Jesuit College and begins his studies to join the Jesuit order.
1666	He is ordained as Father Marquette. He travels to New France as a Jesuit missionary, arriving on September 20.
1668	Father Marquette establishes a mission among the Ottawa Indians at Sault Sainte Marie.
1669	He leaves Sault Sainte Marie for Saint Esprit.
1671	After his mission is raided by bands of Sioux, he leaves Saint Esprit for the mission at Saint Ignace on Lake Michigan.
1672	Governor of New France, Count de Frontenac, appoints Louis Jolliet to find and explore the Mississippi River.
1673	
May 17	The Marquette-Jolliet expedition begins from Saint Ignace.
Early June	Father Marquette visits the Menominee Indians.
June 7	The explorers smoke a peace pipe with the Mascouten Indians.
June 17	The expedition enters the Mississippi River. They visit an Illinois village, where the chief gives Father Marquette a peace pipe for the journey.
Early July	The expedition passes falls at current-day Cairo, Illinois.
July 17	The expedition heads for home.
Late September	They reach the Saint Francis-Xavier mission.
1674	Father Marquette leaves the mission at Saint Francis-Xavier on October 25 for Kaskaskia on the Illinois River.
1675	He finally arrives at Kaskaskia on April 10, after being trapped in the wilderness all winter. Father Marquette dies on May 18.
1677	Ottawa Indians find Father Marquette's bones and return them to the mission at Saint Ignace.

Timeline in History

1534	Jacques Cartier explores the St. Lawrence River and claims the shores of the Gulf of St. Lawrence for France.
1539	Hernando de Soto leads expedition to Florida and inland; he finds the Mississippi River.
1577–1580	Sir Francis Drake circumnavigates the globe.
1587	Colony at Roanoke, Virginia, is established, but soon disappears without explanation.
1588	Spanish Armada attempts to invade England but fails.
1600	Europeans exploit conflicts between Indian nations to secure their fur trade.
1606	Virginia Company receives its charter.
1607	Jamestown, Virginia, is founded.
1608	Samuel de Champlain founds Quebec.
1609	Henry Hudson explores Hudson Bay and River.
1620	Pilgrims arrive at Plymouth.
1624	Treaty of trade is made between Iroquois Indians and New France.
1645	Louis Jolliet is born in Quebec, New France.
1661	Louis XIV becomes King of France.
1668	Louis Jolliet studies cartography and hydrography in France.
1669	Daniel de Rémy, sieur de Courcelle (the governor of New France), sends the first French expedition in search of the Mississippi River.
1674	Louis Jolliet's canoe capsizes, and his original journals and maps of the Mississippi expedition are lost.
1678	Robert de La Salle explores the Mississippi River Valley.
1680	Jolliet receives Anticosti Island in recognition of his achievements.
1682	La Salle claims the Mississippi River for France.
1687	La Salle is murdered by members of his expedition.
1700	Jolliet dies.
1701	Thirty-eight Indian tribes sign a treaty with the French.
1756	The Seven Years' War begins in North America between New France and the British colonies.
1763	Treaty of Paris gives Canada and all the French colonies east of the Mississippi to Britain.

Further Reading

For Young Adults

Donaldson-Forbes, Jeff. *Jacques Marquette and Louis Jolliet.* New York: PowerKids Press, 2002.

Goodman, Joan Elizabeth. *Despite All Obstacles: La Salle and the Conquest of the Mississippi.* New York: Mikaya Press, 2001.

Harmon, Daniel E. *Jolliet and Marquette: Explorers of the Mississippi River.* Topeka, Kansas: Topeka Bindery, 2003.

Larkin, Tanya. *Jacques Marquette and Louis Jolliet: Explorers of the Mississippi.* New York: The Rosen Publishing Group, Inc, 2004.

Lepore, Jill. *Encounters in the New World: A History in Documents.* New York: Oxford University Press, 2000.

Wilbur, Keith C. *Early Explorers of North America.* Philadelphia: Chelsea House Publishers, 1997.

Works Consulted

Donelly, Joseph P., S.J. *Jacques Marquette, S.J.* Chicago: Loyola University Press, 1968.

Marquette, Jacques. *Voyages of Marquette in the Jesuit Relations, 59.* Ann Arbor: University Microfilms, Inc, 1966.

Morgan, Ted. *Wilderness Dawn: The Settling of the North American Continent.* New York: Simon & Shuster, 1993.

Severin, Timothy. *Explorers of the Mississippi.* New York: Alfred A Knopf, 1968.

On the Internet

Dictionary of Canadian Biography Online
  http://www.biographi.ca/index2.html

Explorers of the Millennium: Marquette and Joliet
  http://library.thinkquest.org/4034/marquettejolliet.html

France in America
  http://memory.loc.gov/intldl/fiahtml/fiatheme.html#track1

Jacques Marquette
  http://www.elizabethan-era.org.uk/jacques-marquette.htm

Journal of Father Jacques Marquette
  http://www.encyclopedia.chicagohistory.org/pages/10873.html

Glossary

astrolabe (AS-troh-layb)—A medieval instrument explorers used to determine the altitude of the sun or other celestial bodies.

birchbark (BIRCH-bark)—Peeled bark of the paper birch tree.

calumet (KAL-yoo-met)—A peace pipe. An area of northeast Illinois and northwest Indiana has been named Calumet.

cartography (kar-TAH-gruh-fee)—The art of making maps or charts.

college (KAH-lidj)—An institution of higher learning. Jacques Marquette attended a Jesuit college, which was the equivalent of modern-day grades three through twelve.

conquistador (kon-KEE-stah-dor)—A Spanish soldier, explorer, or adventurer of the fifteenth to seventeenth centuries.

dysentery (DIS-en-tayr-ee)—An infectious disease that causes severe diarrhea.

fluent (FLOO-ent)—Able to speak well.

hydrography (hy-DRAH-gruh-fee)—The mapping of bodies of water.

Jesuit (JEH-zhoo-it)—A religious order of Roman Catholic priests founded by Saint Ignatius Loyola.

mission (MIH-shun)—A place where missionaries live and work while in the field.

missionary (MIH-shuh-nay-ree)—A religious person sent to minister and care for others.

novitiate (noh-VIH-shee-it)—1. A novice (a person new to an activity). Jacques Marquette was a novitiate Jesuit while studying to become a priest. 2. The period of being a novice. 3. The place where novices live.

pilgrimage (PIL-gruh-midj)—A journey to a sacred place or shrine.

sagamite (SAH-juh-myt)—A mush made of boiled Indian corn, seasoned with fat.

sailcloth (SAYL-kloth)—Heavy cotton canvas used for making sails and tents.

scholastic (skuh-LAS-tik)—A Jesuit student who has taken his vows but has not been ordained as a priest.

scurvy (SKUR-vee)—A disease caused by a vitamin C deficiency.

shallop (SHAL-up)—A large heavy boat used to sail in shallow waters.

tributary (TRIH-byoo-tayr-ee)—A stream or river that flows into a larger waterway.

typhoid (TY-foid)—A disease that causes fever, diarrhea, and severe headaches.

voyageur (VOY-uh-zhur)—A woodsman, boatman, or guide employed by a fur company to transport goods and supplies.

watershed (WAH-ter-shed)—The region that drains water into a river or other body of water.

Index